Pupil Book 4

Vocabulary, Grammar and Punctuation

Author: Abigail Steel

William Collins' dream of knowledge for all began with the publication of his first book in 1819. A self-educated mill worker, he not only enriched millions of lives, but also founded a flourishing publishing house. Today, staying true to this spirit, Collins books are packed with inspiration, innovation and practical expertise. They place you at the centre of a world of possibility and give you exactly what you need to explore it.

Collins. Freedom to teach.

Published by Collins
An imprint of HarperCollins*Publishers*
The News Building
1 London Bridge Street
London
SE1 9GF

Browse the complete Collins catalogue at
www.collins.co.uk

10 9 8 7 6 5 4 3 2 1

ISBN 978-0-00-813333-7

British Library Cataloguing in Publication Data
A Catalogue record for this publication is available from the British Library

Edited by Hannah Hirst-Dunton
Cover design and artwork by Amparo Barrera
Internal design concept by Amparo Barrera
Typesetting by Jouve India Private Ltd
Illustrations by Eva Morales, Dante Ginevra, Aptara and QBS

Printed in Italy by Grafica Veneta S.p.A.

Pupil Book 4
Vocabulary, Grammar and Punctuation

Contents

Dictionary definitions

A **definition** is the meaning of a word. You can use a **dictionary** to find the definitions of words, along with some other information about them.

- For the word **bed**:
  bed noun
  a piece of furniture used for sleeping
  (plural **beds**)

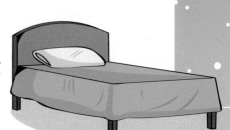

- For the word **breathe**:
  breathe verb (pronounced breeth)
  to take air into your lungs and send it out again
  (**breathes, breathing, breathed**)

Get started

Look up the words in the box using a dictionary. Then copy and complete each dictionary definition using the correct word. One has been done for you.

precious   optician   suspicious   ignite   anxious   barricade

1. <u>suspicious</u>: *unsure and doubtful*

2. _____: a person who makes glasses and contact lenses

3. _____: of great value

4. _____: worried or nervous

5. _____: a barrier, especially one blocking a street

6. _____: to set fire to

Try these

Look up each word in a dictionary and write down the definition you find. One has been done for you.

1. exclude: *to leave someone or something out*

2. partial

3. journalist

4. dependent

5. fledgling

6. abominable

7. originate

8. exclaim

Now try these

Write your own definitions for these terms in the style of a dictionary entry. Use a dictionary for help if you need to, but try to use your own words.

1. apple

2. lion

3. shout

4. jump

5. colourful

6. heavy

Using a dictionary

Dictionaries give us the **definitions** of words, along with some other information about them. Some words have more than one definition.

> For the word **example**:
>
> **example** noun (pronounced ex-**am**-pul / ex-**ahm**-pul)
>
> 1. a single thing or event that shows what others of the same kind are like
>
>   For example: The play we are reading is a good example of a tragedy.
>
> 2. a person or thing that you should copy or from which you could learn
>
>   For example: Timothy is acting as an example to us all.
>
>   (plural **examples**)

Get started

Look up each word in a dictionary. Find and write down the word that comes **after** it, with its definition. One has been done for you.

1. juggernaut

   Answer: *juggle: to keep throwing a number of objects into the air and catching them, without dropping any*

2. incapable   3. secret   4. librarian

5. edible   6. flexible   7. quarrel

8. inquire

Try these

Look up each word in a dictionary. Write it down, with its part of speech and two different meanings that you find. One has been done for you.

1. pride

Answer: *pride, noun: 1) a group of lions*
                        2) a feeling of satisfaction

2. inseparable

3. organic

4. company

5. interfere

6. date

7. pupil

8. improvise

Now try these

Look up each word in a dictionary and use it in a sentence of your own.

1. impulsive

2. hubbub

3. gingerly

4. flustered

5. contemplate

6. flinch

Word families (1)

Just like people, words can have families! **Word families** are groups of words that are related in some way. Many word families are related by the same **root word**.

- Root word **light**: lightly, lightweight, lighthouse, lightning

- Root word **drop**: dropping, droplet, dropped, raindrop

Get started

Copy and complete each word family by adding three more words to the root word. Use a dictionary for help if you need to. One has been done for you.

1. *paint: painter, painting, painted*

2. help:

3. jump:

4. play:

5. post:

6. count:

7. think:

8. ground:

Try these

Copy and complete these sentences using the words from the **like** family in the box. Use a dictionary for help if you need to. One has been done for you.

likely	likelihood	likeness	likeable	childlike	liking

1. It is <u>likely</u> that I will have school dinner every day this week.

2. Gabriella was so excited that she clapped her hands with _____ glee.

3. I have developed a strong _____ for dark chocolate – it's delicious!

4. There is a real _____ that we have a times tables test tomorrow.

5. The new boy in our class is very _____.

6. People say my sister and I have a close _____ to one another.

Now try these

Write two sentences for each root word using at least two different words from its word family. Use a dictionary for help if you need to.

1. Root word **work**: working, worker, workshop, teamwork
2. Root word **time**: timer, timing, timed, overtime
3. Root word **dream**: dreaming, dreamer, daydream, dreamy
4. Root word **drop**: dropping, droplet, dropped, raindrop
5. Root word **pay**: paying, payment, repaid, underpaid
6. Root word **solve**: solver, solving, solution, dissolve

Word families (2)

Just like people, words can have families! **Word families** are groups of words that are related in some way. Many word families are related by the same **root word**, but they don't always look the same. When you are trying to work out whether words belong to the same family, think about the meanings as well as the look of words.

- Root word **shine**: shiny, shining, shone, sunshine
- Root word **glass**: glassy, glaze, glazier, double-glazing

Get started

Use your dictionary to write a definition for each of these words from the **serve** family. One has been done for you.

1. *servant: a person who performs duties for others*

2. service:

3. reservation:

4. server:

5. serving:

6. servile:

7. subservience:

8. serve:

Try these

Copy and complete these sentences using words from the **light** word family. You may wish to use a dictionary for help and note down the word family first. One has been done for you.

1. *It was a stormy night and, with a deafening noise, <u>lightning</u> hit the tree.*

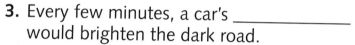

2. The ships at sea looked for the _____ to guide them to shore.

3. Every few minutes, a car's _____ would brighten the dark road.

4. Joel's dad was standing on a chair, trying to change the broken _____.

5. It was midnight and Archie was asleep, but we could see by the _____ gleaming down from the night sky.

6. Sophia ran her fingertips _____ over the furry coat – it was so soft.

7. I chose a yellow _____ from my pencil case to pick out the key words on the page.

8. My bag was really heavy, so mum took out the water bottle to _____ the load.

Now try these

Write one sentence for each of these words from the **play** family. Use a dictionary for help if you like.

1. playground
2. replayed
3. player
4. playful
5. playwright
6. screenplay

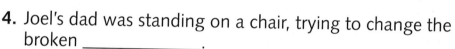

Nouns with prefixes

A **prefix** is a group of letters that can be added to the beginning of a word to change its meaning. There are lots of prefixes you can add to nouns to create new nouns.

- **mis-** = bad / incorrect
- **dis-** = not / lack of
- **inter-** = between
- **sub-** = under / below
- **super-** / **over-** = bigger / more than usual

- **anti-** = against
- **auto-** = self / on its own
- **ex-** = not any more
- **co-** = with
- **micro-** / **mini-** = small

Get started

Look at each word's prefix. Try to write a definition for the word on your own, before using a dictionary for help. Then put the word into a sentence. One has been done for you.

1. misfortune

    Answer: *Misfortune is bad fortune or bad luck. Black cats bring misfortune — to mice!*

2. supermarket

3. disorganisation

4. antifreeze

5. autopilot

6. ex-soldier

7. microchip

8. minibus

Try these

Copy and complete these sentences by adding a prefix from the box. Use a dictionary for help if you need to. One has been done for you.

anti	dis	over	sub	super	inter

1. The film had a really terrible ending — it was such an __anti__ climax.

2. What's that flying through the air? It's a _____ hero!

3. Our teacher likes us to chat about our work in big groups, so there's a lot of _____ action in the classroom.

4. The _____ appearance of my watch is a mystery I still haven't solved.

5. The road was busy so we took the _____ way under the street.

6. Hannah was completely exhausted: she was suffering from _____ work.

Now try these

Use a dictionary to find a new noun that contains each of these prefixes and use it in a sentence. One has been done for you.

1. inter-

   Answer: *interview*

   My brother Henri had an interview for university last week.

2. intra-   3. multi-

4. techno-   5. dis-

Standard English word choices

Standard English is different from formal language – it simply means correct spelling and grammar. Many people use **non-Standard English** in speech.

- Non-Standard English: I don't want **no** help.
- Standard English: I don't want **any** help.

Get started

Copy out these sentences, underlining the words that indicate non-Standard English. One has been done for you.

1. *It wasn't me <u>what</u> did it.*

2. That's a lotta work they gave us.

3. I didn't do it – I haven't done nothing!

4. My lil sister just won't stop following me around!

5. As soon as we get home we can have a nice cuppa tea.

6. Yeah, I'd love to come!

7. He's a smelly ol dog, but I like him.

8. I luv that film – LOL!

Try these

Copy and complete each sentence, adding the Standard English word from the box. One has been done for you.

1. *I haven't been doing <u>anything</u> all day – just sitting here!*

2. Will you pass _____ glass over, please?

3. The rules aren't too hard now, _____ we learned them last week.

4. There's quite a _____ pressure on me to pass the test tomorrow.

5. I think it was the big dog _____ broke the vase.

6. Would _____ like to come swimming with me?

anything / nothing
my / me
cos / because
lotta / lot of
what / that
y'all / you

Now try these

Write a short letter in Standard English for each of the reasons below. Pay close attention to your word choices. Swap your letter with a partner's and discuss your word choices together.

1. An invitation to a friend to come to a party.

2. A letter to a family member, telling them a piece of news.

3. A letter to one of your parents, as though you are apart for a week or two.

4. A postcard to a brother or sister.

5. A chatty letter to a friend you haven't seen for a while.

Parts of speech

Words in sentences can be divided, according to their purpose, into groups called **parts of speech**. Three parts of speech are **adjectives**, **nouns** and **verbs**.

- The squirrel (noun) climbs (verb) a large (adjective) tree (noun).

- The girl (noun) brushes (verb) her red (adjective) hair (noun).

Get started

Copy out each sentence, underlining and labelling the adjectives, nouns and verbs in each one. One has been done for you.

1. The little birds are sitting on the spindly branches.

   adjective noun verb verb   adjective noun

2. A large, black bird startles the smaller birds.

3. The black bird flies away to eat bread in the big city.

4. The city is busy, loud and dangerous to visit.

5. The large black bird feels small next to the huge buildings.

6. The old, dry food he finds tastes horrid.

7. The black bird flies back to his leafy home in the quiet countryside.

8. He becomes friendly with the little birds living in the trees.

Try these

Copy and complete these sentences by adding a suitable noun.
One has been done for you.

1. *When I am daydreaming, I look out of the* <u>*window*</u>.
2. From our back garden, I can see lots of _____.
3. Five little _____ ran happily through the park.
4. Brendan awoke and opened his _____.
5. I'll put on my _____ because it's very chilly today.
6. After school, I will have _____.
7. The _____ is my favourite type of animal.
8. Quickly, I looked for my _____.

Now try these

Copy and complete these sentences by adding a
suitable verb. One has been done for you.

1. *The squirrels* <u>*jump*</u> *through the
   trees without falling once.*
2. From where I sat, I watched a boy _____
   along the riverbank with his mother.
3. I always enjoy _____ with my friends –
   I can't wait until next time I see them.
4. We _____ at school today, and I really enjoyed it.
5. The dogs _____ in the park with their owners.
6. All of a sudden, my big sister _____.

Sentences and phrases

A **sentence** is a group of words that makes sense on its own. Every sentence needs a verb. A **phrase** is a group of words that does not make complete sense on its own. Phrases never contain a subject doing the action of a verb.

- Sentence: The girl ran.

- Phrase: The girl with short hair

- Phrase: Running quickly over the beach

Get started

Copy out each example and label it 'sentence' or 'phrase'. One has been done for you.

1. *The sun shone.* sentence

2. In the clear, blue sky without a single cloud

3. Dogs barked and yapped.

4. They chased seagulls.

5. Dashing in and out of the choppy waves with white crests

6. The small, yapping dog

7. There was a large, elaborate sandcastle on the beach.

8. The broken sandcastle that had been knocked down by the dogs.

Try these

Copy and complete these sentences by adding a phrase to give extra information. One has been done for you.

1. *The family unpacked their picnic on a beautiful, sandy beach.*

2. A gentle breeze blew . . .

3. The children looked for crabs . . .

4. They found some little fish . . .

5. They built a sandcastle . . .

6. After exploring, the children sat down to eat . . .

7. It was a delicious picnic . . .

8. All in all, everyone thought they had . . .

Now try these

Use each of these phrases to write your own sentence.

1. the grassy path through the pretty forest

2. after the warm spring rain

3. hurrying past the Saturday shoppers

4. a river that glistened in the moonlight

5. in a draughty old barn

6. completely ruining the surprise

Noun phrases

A **noun phrase** is a group of words that acts as a **noun**. The noun itself is the most important word in the phrase. In a simple noun phrase, the noun comes after a **determiner**.

- Noun: horse

- Noun phrase: A horse

- Determiners: a, an, the, this, that, these, some, those, our, my, her, his, its, your, their

Get started

Copy out these sentences, underlining the noun phrases in each one. One has been done for you.

1. <u>His prisoner</u> successfully escaped <u>the dungeon</u>.

2. My aunt will take me shopping in a minute.

3. We wanted to go out, and decided to visit that castle by those mountains.

4. These pears don't taste anywhere near as good as those from our tree.

5. For your birthday, Chrissie and Frankie wrapped their present carefully.

6. Outside, her dog ran around chasing its tail.

7. Ferdie picked an apple from his garden for lunch.

8. Some vegetables always form part of my dinner.

Try these

Copy and complete these sentences by adding a determiner before each noun. Try to use a different determiner each time. One has been done for you.

1. *We went for a long walk in __the__ hills.*

2. I could see that _____ dog was having a great time.

3. At lunchtime I sat down to eat _____ sandwiches.

4. After those, I ate _____ orange, which was juicy.

5. In the afternoon, we told _____ stories as we walked.

6. Mum kept losing _____ hat in the wind!

7. Dad tied it on for her with _____ scarf.

8. _____ days out are always lots of fun.

Now try these

Copy and complete these sentences by adding simple noun phrases.

1. After a long time searching, we found . . .

2. We hoped we might see . . .

3. We explored carefully all over . . .

4. We finally exhausted ourselves and sat down for . . .

5. We ran most of the way back to . . .

6. Gratefully, we warmed up in front of . . .

Using pronouns to make your writing clear

Pronouns take the place of nouns and help us to avoid repetition.

- Repetitive: Barney put on **Barney's** hat and waved goodbye to **Barney's** mum.

- Clearer: Barney put on **his** hat and waved goodbye to **his** mum.

However, sometimes using pronouns can also become confusing.

- Unclear: Ross wanted to talk to Mr Clark, but **he** was too busy.

- Clear: Ross wanted to talk to Mr Clark, but **Ross** was too busy.

Get started

Copy and complete these sentences by adding different pronouns. One has been done for you.

1. *Donna fetched __her__ winter clothes.*

2. _____ found a scarf and gloves.

3. There was also a hat – _____ were all different colours.

4. Zeke fetched _____ coat.

5. _____ was red, with toggles.

6. Zeke's uncle handed an umbrella to _____.

7. Donna, Zeke and I left the house – _____ were going walking.

8. Would _____ like to come with _____?

Try these

Copy out each sentence and label it 'clear' or 'unclear' to show whether or not the pronoun is clear in its meaning. If it is unclear, suggest an alternative word. One has been done for you.

1. *Ajay and Felix set up <u>his</u> train track. unclear: Ajay's*

2. Ajay got out the train and lined up <u>its</u> carriages.

3. Ajay asked Shirley to join <u>him</u>.

4. Shirley asked her sister and <u>she</u> said no.

5. Felix looked from the girls to the carriages: he couldn't understand <u>them</u>.

6. Shirley's sister walked away and <u>she</u> looked confused.

Now try these

Rewrite these sentences, replacing some of the names with pronouns. If a pronoun would be confusing, don't replace the name.

1. Mathias took off Mathias' muddy wellies and put on Mathias' slippers.

2. Elodie washed Elodie's face and brushed Elodie's teeth.

3. Adesh and Adesh's mother struggled to remove Adesh's coat.

4. Laurie wanted to go out, but Laurie's friend thought Laurie would rather watch a film.

Adverbs and adverbials

An **adverb** is a word that **adds meaning** to a verb. Adverbs can tell you how, when or where the verb was happening. Sometimes we use an **adverbial phrase** or **adverbial clause** that acts as an adverb.

- The bear lives **under the stairs**.

- Janine woke up **the next morning**.

Get started

Copy out these sentences, underlining the adverbials. One has been done for you.

1. *Robbie ran <u>like a rocket</u>!*

2. Augustus practised all day long.

3. Hazel swam every morning.

4. Prema spoke with a grumpy tone.

5. Carys climbed up the old oak tree.

6. Arjun walked into the nearest town.

7. We heard a strange noise late at night.

8. Someone spilled juice all over my book.

Try these

Copy and complete each sentence, adding the most appropriate adverbial from the box. One has been done for you.

> | very tunefully indeed | as quickly as I could | with lots of colours |
> | when we went to the library | in the petting zoo | at the zoo keeper |

1. We danced _to the music_.
2. The lion growled _____.
3. I stroked the rabbit _____.
4. We got a treat because we behaved _____.
5. I tidied my bedroom _____.
6. Tracey painted _____.

Now try these

Copy and complete these sentences by adding adverbials of your own. One has been done for you.

1. _My mum goes to a book club on the first Monday of every month._
2. Our bins get collected . . .
3. We went out for a family meal . . .
4. I learned my lines . . .
5. The car raced away . . .
6. We planned a day out . . .

Fronted adverbials

An **adverbial** is a word, phrase or clause that **adds meaning** to a verb. Adverbials can tell you how, when or where the verb was happening.

If we put the adverbial at the front of the sentence, it is called a **fronted adverbial**. Fronted adverbials can make sentences more atmospheric.

- **That night**, something serious happened.
- **When all the guards were asleep**, the lion escaped.

Get started

Copy out these sentences and underline the fronted adverbials. One has been done for you.

1. <u>In the darkness</u>, the lion had climbed a tree and got out.

2. At first, the zookeeper couldn't believe his eyes.

3. Finally, he had to raise the alarm.

4. In the morning, the town was in chaos!

5. Before breakfast, everyone was out in the streets.

6. Because of the escape, sirens were wailing.

7. Through the dense fog, officials searched high and low.

8. By a stroke of luck, Mr Federer found a clue.

Try these

Copy out each sentence, moving the adverbial phrase to make it a fronted adverbial. One has been done for you.

1. We had visited the zoo the day before.

    Answer: *The day before, we had visited the zoo.*

2. We had seen the lion staring at us through the glass of his enclosure.

3. He had been pacing around looking bored.

4. He looked very old when he gazed out at us.

5. I bet he'd not been outside in his whole life.

6. There wasn't much to do in his cage.

7. He had finally decided to escape for an adventure.

8. I felt sorry for him deep down.

Now try these

Copy and complete these sentences by adding fronted adverbials.

1. ... Mr Federer noticed a muddy footprint.

2. ... he gathered a team of zoo keepers.

3. ... they set off to track down the beast.

4. ... the sound of the lion snoring drifted out.

5. ... they hatched a fool-proof plan.

6. ... they lured the sleepy lion out towards the van.

Revising conjunctions

Conjunctions are words that join two clauses together in a sentence. Sometimes conjunctions can be used at the **beginnings** of sentences.

- Sima went to the zoo **where** she saw some giraffes.

- **Because** they are her favourite animals, this made her happy.

Get started

Copy and complete these sentences by adding suitable conjunctions. Try to use a different conjunction in each one. One has been done for you.

1. Sima's family went to the zoo __*and*__ they had a great time.

2. They set off early _____ they were still late arriving.

3. _____ it was a busy Saturday, the car park was full.

4. They collected their tickets _____ they went to see the animals.

5. _____ there were not lots of other people, the zoo wasn't too crowded.

6. They could visit the insect house _____ they wanted to see bugs.

7. They could go to a sea-lion show _____ they could watch the trained monkeys.

8. _____ they saw a huge crocodile, Sima's brother shuddered.

Try these

Join each pair of sentences together using a suitable conjunction. Try to use a different conjunction in each one. One has been done for you.

1. Sima enjoyed the sea-lion show. Ahmed preferred the lions.

   Answer: *Sima enjoyed the sea-lion show but Ahmed preferred the lions.*

2. They both liked the elephants. They loved the kangaroos.

3. They stopped for lunch. They had an ice-cream.

4. Ahmed felt disappointed. The tigers were hiding.

5. It would have been thrilling. He had seen them.

6. The children were full of energy. It was a long day.

7. They bought souvenirs from the gift shop. They left to go home.

8. They wanted to get mementos. They had had such a good day.

Now try these

Copy and complete these sentences by adding a conjunction and another main clause. Think carefully about which conjunction best gives the meaning you want.

1. The monkey was funny . . .

2. The rhinoceros was massive . . .

3. Apes are very clever . . .

4. My favourites are the water animals . . .

5. My brother loves the big cats . . .

Conjunctions to express time and cause

Subordinating conjunctions can give information about **time** (what happened when) and **cause** (the reasons behind something).

- Time: I got home **when** mum was leaving.

- Cause: I got into trouble **because** I flicked a pea at Sophie.

While, **since** and **as** can give information about either, in different sentences!

Get started

Copy out each sentence, underlining the conjunction. Then label the sentence 'time' or 'cause' to show what information the conjunction gives. One has been done for you.

1. I'll put on my coat <u>after</u> I've laced up my shoes. time

2. We went shopping before we went to the cinema.

3. So I can go to the party, I've done my homework.

4. I've been busy as Mum is poorly at the moment.

5. I hid in my bedroom when Dad said we should go.

6. While I brushed my hair, I chatted on the phone.

7. I opened the classroom door as the bell was ringing.

8. Our match was cancelled as there was a storm.

Try these

Copy and complete these sentences, adding a suitable conjunction that shows time or cause, as indicated. One has been done for you.

1. Time: *We went to a toyshop __while__ Dad went for coffee.*

2. Time: I wanted the new game _____ I saw an advert.

3. Time: I grabbed the last one _____ it sold out.

4. Time: _____ the moment I got the game, I've wanted to play it.

5. Cause: I rushed to get home _____ I needed my computer.

6. Cause: The bus was late _____ the traffic is bad.

7. Cause: I read the instructions _____ I could get started.

8. Cause: Dad offered to help me set up _____ he knew I was excited.

Now try these

Copy and complete these sentences, adding a conjunction and clause to show time or cause, as indicated.

1. Time: My sister annoyed me . . .

2. Time: I'll do more around the house . . .

3. Time: I stayed up late . . .

4. Cause: We packed a suitcase . . .

5. Cause: I have to get changed . . .

6. Cause: I was rushing around . . .

Plural or possessive?

At the end of most plural nouns, we add a letter **s** with no apostrophe. To show possession, we use an apostrophe and the letter **s** at the end of a singular noun. At the end of a plural noun that already ends in **s**, we add only the apostrophe.

- Plural: cats (more than one cat)

- Singular possessive: cat's bed (a bed that belongs to one cat)

- Plural possessive: cats' bed (a bed that belongs to more than one cat)

Get started

Copy out each sentence and label it 'correct' or 'incorrect' to show whether or not apostrophes have been used correctly. One has been done for you.

1. My sister and I have two new kitten's.
   incorrect

2. My sister's kitten is called Ginger.

3. My kitten's paws are white.

4. Our two kitten's have red bowls.

5. I chose both of the two kittens' collars.

6. The collars' are the same colour but have different patterns.

7. The main colour of both pattern's is purple.

8. The two sisters' two kittens' collars are purple.

Try these

Copy and correct these sentences by removing the apostrophes that are not needed to show possession. One has been done for you.

1. My sister's friend Harry has three hamster's.

   Answer: *My sister's friend Harry has three hamsters.*

2. The hamsters' gnaw on his carpet.

3. All of his hamsters' have sharp teeth.

4. Harry must watch his hamsters' closely.

5. Harry's two brothers' are unhelpful.

6. His brothers' cheer on the little pet's.

7. Harry's hamsters' are very naughty.

8. However, his brother's think the hamsters' antics' are funny.

Now try these

Copy and complete these sentences by adding apostrophes where needed.

1. I saw my two friends rabbits in their new hutches.

2. The rabbits hutches are huge.

3. Sarahs favourite walk is to visit the horses.

4. The doors of the horses stables creak loudly.

5. The twins parrots live at their mums house.

6. The parrots squawks are muffled by her houses thick walls.

Paragraphs (1)

Paragraphs make a long piece of writing easier to read. One paragraph is a group of sentences about one idea or topic.

Get started

Copy out each sentence about paragraphs. Then label it 'true' or 'false' to show whether or not it is correct. One has been done for you.

1. *Paragraphs can help with clarity in long pieces of writing.   true*

2. One paragraph contains one sentence.

3. One paragraph is about one idea or topic.

4. There must be at least seven paragraphs in every piece of writing.

5. Paragraphs must start with bullet points.

6. You should start a new paragraph when you change the subject.

7. You could start a new paragraph when you introduce a new character, time or setting.

8. The main point of a paragraph is to help slow the reader down.

Try these

Write one paragraph for each topic. Use at least four sentences in each paragraph, and remember that all of the sentences in one paragraph should be about the same idea. One has been done for you.

1. Favourite games

    I have three favourite games — tag, hide-and-seek and stuck-in-the-mud. They are all fun because you run around. I like stuck-in-the-mud the most as you play in teams. This is good because I like playing more than I enjoy a competition.

2. Wild animals

3. A current school project

4. Your last holiday

5. One of your friends

Now try these

Write a short paragraph for each heading in this story plan. Use at least three sentences in each paragraph.

1. Opening: Describe an imaginary underwater setting

2. Build up: Describe your main character

3. Problem: Your character is worried because humans are polluting the sea

4. Challenge: Your character must decide how to stop them

5. Resolution: A new friend helps out and the plan succeeds

6. Ending: Describe the underwater party celebrating your character's success!

Paragraphs (2)

Paragraphs make long pieces of writing easier to read. One paragraph is about one idea or topic.

Get started

Look at this passage about a school play. It has not been split into paragraphs.

> This term we are rehearsing a play. Rehearsals are every Tuesday. They're run by Mrs Barrowman. I signed up straight away, and I enjoy rehearsals very much. The school orchestra is learning the songs for the play. There are lots of violin solos in the song I sing, so they are practising hard. My song is about getting dressed for the ball. The costumes in the play are being made by parents. My friend's mum, Dr Kenza, is in charge of costumes. My mum is making me some glittery wings. The play will be performed in front of all the parents and teachers. During the performances, the children not acting will help out backstage. We are all very excited about finally putting on the play.

1. How many different subjects related to the school play does this passage cover?

2. Imagine you are going to split the passage into paragraphs about these different subjects. What sentence should start the second paragraph?

3. What is the topic of this second paragraph?

4. What sentence should start the third paragraph?

5. What is the topic of this third paragraph?

6. What sentence should start the fourth paragraph?

7. What is the topic of this fourth paragraph?

8. What effect does splitting the passage like this have?

Try these

For each topic heading, write three ideas for different paragraphs. One has been done for you.

1. Sharks

   Answer: *What types there are; where they live; what they eat*

2. Using a computer

3. Helping others

4. Crocodiles

5. Countries to visit

6. A day at school

7. After-school clubs

8. Being healthy

Now try these

For each topic heading, plan four short paragraphs on different ideas. Write the first one or two sentences of each paragraph to show what it will be about.

1. Charity shops

2. Leisure centres

3. Parks

4. The circus

5. The cinema

6. Fun places in your town

Standard and non-Standard verbs (I)

Standard English is different from formal language – it simply means correct spelling and grammar. Many people use non-Standard English in speech.

- Non-Standard English: I **is** busy.

- Standard English: I **am** busy.

Get started

Copy out the sentence from each pair that does **not** use Standard English. One has been done for you.

1. **a)** I ain't worried 'bout t' game.

   b) I'm not worried about the game.

   Answer: *I ain't worried 'bout t' game.*

2. **a)** I am feeling focused.

   b) I is feelin' focused.

3. **a)** I wasn't thinking about anything except winning.

   b) I weren't thinking 'bout nothing 'cept winning.

4. **a)** I could of relaxed a bit anyways.

   b) I could have relaxed a bit anyway.

5. **a)** You've never thought it through.

   b) Yous lot 've never thinked it through.

Try these

Copy out these sentences, underlining the non-Standard verbs. One has been done for you.

1. *I was <u>sat</u> waiting when the bus arrived.*

2. Where are you gan, Granddad?

3. To go with her costume, she were wearing a mask.

4. I's coming – wait a moment!

5. It's freezing today, innit?

6. Before we go, I be finishing my homework.

7. We walked out into the rain – we was soaked!

8. José could of come, but he'd forgotten.

Now try these

Copy and complete each sentence, adding the Standard English verb from the box.

1. Yesterday, we _____ discussing Sports Day in class.

2. My friends _____ very bothered about the relay.

3. I _____ feeling a bit anxious about it.

4. They thought I _____ being silly.

5. They _____ teasing me all afternoon!

6. I could _____ been annoyed, but I laughed with them.

was / were
ain't / aren't
am / is
was / were
been / have been
have / of

Standard and non-Standard verbs (2)

Standard English is different from formal language – it simply means correct spelling and grammar. Many people use non-Standard English in speech.

- Non-standard English: The dog **digged** a hole.

- Standard English: The dog **dug** a hole.

Get started

Rewrite each sentence, replacing the underlined non-Standard English verb with a Standard English verb. One has been done for you.

1. Mrs Choudhary <u>taked</u> us to the museum.

   Answer: *Mrs Choudhary <u>took</u> us to the museum.*

2. We <u>ain't</u> been to it before.

3. I was <u>sat</u> next to Josie on the bus.

4. I <u>is</u> fascinated by dinosaurs.

5. I <u>weren't</u> expecting them to be so big!

6. Josie <u>don't</u> usually enjoy school trips.

7. This time, though, she <u>speaked</u> about it all the way home.

8. We could <u>of</u> stayed all day.

Try these

Rewrite each sentence, identifying the non-Standard English verb and replacing it with a Standard English verb. One has been done for you.

1. We ain't enjoyed a day out this much in ages.

   Answer: *We haven't enjoyed a day out this much in ages.*

2. I showed Josie a woolly mammoth and she find a spider that was bigger than her hand!

3. The guides been telling us a lot of facts, and they were great.

4. If I'd know them already, I'd have felt really clever.

5. I'd of told everyone I know!

6. At lunch, we ate our food and drinked our juice in the café.

7. There were even a dinosaur in there!

8. We didn't get to see everything, so we just got to go back one day soon.

Now try these

Copy and complete these sentences by adding Standard English verbs.

1. The school trip _____ a huge success.

2. We _____ going to forget it for a long time.

3. I _____ still really excited that I saw an Egyptian mummy.

4. Even Josie _____ around in excitement.

5. We would _____ stayed later if we could.

6. We each wrote a report on what we _____.

Commas after fronted adverbials

If we put an adverbial at the front of the sentence, it is called a **fronted adverbial.** We always put a **comma** after a fronted adverbial.

- On Tuesday, we went to visit the old castle.

- After visiting the castle, the children ate lunch.

Get started

Copy and complete these sentences, adding commas after the fronted adverbials. One has been done for you.

1. *Listening to the tour, the children learned about the castle's history.*

2. Long ago the castle had been made from wood.

3. Unfortunately a lot of the wood was destroyed in a fire.

4. As a result they needed to use a stronger material.

5. From the finest stone the castle had been rebuilt.

6. From that day to this it has remained unchanged.

7. By the end of the tour everyone was fascinated.

8. Clearly they couldn't wait to see more.

Try these

Copy out these sentences, which do **not** contain any commas. Label each sentence 'fronted' or 'not fronted' to show where its adverbial phrase is positioned. Then add commas after the fronted adverbials. One has been done for you.

1. After the tour the children explored.

   Answer: *fronted: After the tour, the children explored.*

2. They went separate ways after a while.

3. Surprisingly there was even more to learn about the castle.

4. Hundreds of years ago the castle had been a thriving community.

5. It was left in ruins only after World War 2.

6. Before that it had been converted for army training.

7. As they got on the bus the children chattered.

8. They wrote thank-you letters once they'd got back to school.

Now try these

Copy and complete these sentences by adding fronted adverbials with commas.

1. … there was a small animal sanctuary.

2. … we saw rabbits.

3. … the rabbits were jumping around.

4. … I approached them.

5. … they were quite friendly.

Apostrophes to show possession (1)

To show possession, we use an apostrophe and the letter **s** at the end of a singular noun. At the end of a plural noun that already ends in **s**, we add only the apostrophe.

- Singular possessive: the boy's T-shirt (the T-shirt that belongs to one boy)

- Plural possessive: the chickens' eggs (the eggs that belong to more than one chicken)

Get started

Copy out these sentences, underlining the words that use plural possessive apostrophes. One has been done for you.

1. *Ella went to visit Duncan's <u>ponies</u>' stables.*

2. The boy's T-shirts' colours had all faded in the wash.

3. Near the library's open window, the books' covers had been soaked with rain.

4. The teacher's folder was bursting full of work for her pupils' lessons.

5. The lunchbox's different compartments' corners were all full of crumbs.

6. Kelly's mum refilled their cats' bowls.

7. The cup cakes' icing had run over the plate's edge.

8. The girls' group's painting had won the school prize.

Try these

Copy and complete these sentences by adding apostrophes showing possession to the underlined plural words. One has been done for you.

1. Both <u>jackets</u>' buttons were large and black.

2. The <u>sisters</u> toy box needed cleaning out.

3. My two <u>cousins</u> parrot is hilarious.

4. Mrs Peacock displayed the <u>groups</u> artwork.

5. The dirty <u>trousers</u> pockets were full of sand.

6. There was mud all over the pair of <u>shoes</u> soles.

7. All the <u>cars</u> headlights were flashing through the rain.

8. Our three <u>friends</u> favourite films are all comedies.

Now try these

Change each example into a phrase that uses a plural possessive apostrophe (for example, the oranges' peel) and use it in a sentence of your own.

1. the ice-creams belonging to the ladies

2. the pram belonging to the babies

3. the nest of the ants

4. the bowls belonging to the dogs

5. the smell of the pies

6. the wrapping paper of the presents

Apostrophes to show possession (2)

To show possession with a plural noun that does **not** end in **s**, we use an apostrophe **and** the letter **s** – just like after a singular noun.

- Possessive singular: the boy's T-shirt

- Possessive plural with **s**: the chickens' eggs

- Possessive plural without **s**: the children's sweets

Get started

Copy out each sentence and label it 'correct' or 'incorrect' to show whether **all** the apostrophes have been used correctly. One has been done for you.

1. *Pupils' families were included in the school's invitation to the children's exhibition.* correct

2. Tabithas' three cats' plan was to wait outside the mices' holes.

3. Shania's lunch was scrambled eggs, which had bits of the eggs' shell in it.

4. Both men's cars' seats were dirty.

5. The girls' friend went out for pasta, and the chef's dishes' flavours were remarkable.

6. Jo's feets' blisters needed the plasters' cushioning.

Try these

Copy and complete these sentences by adding possessive apostrophes in the correct places. One has been done for you.

1. _Children's pictures will be included in my school's yearbook._

2. The mens plan was to see the museums new display.

3. All these hot drinks dark colour affects your teeths brightness.

4. The five sheeps fields grass was cut too short.

5. The geeses nest was even bigger than our two ducks nest.

6. The mices plan was to sneak out and eat the three cats dinners!

7. The ladys old age made her careful of her feets comfort.

8. Gwens shopping trip took us to three departments: Toys, Gifts and Womens Clothing.

Now try these

Turn each noun into a plural possessive phrase that uses an apostrophe. Finally, use this phrase in a sentence of your own.

1. mouse

2. woman

3. child

4. foot

5. tooth

6. goose

Punctuating direct speech (1)

When we write the words that someone has said, this is **direct speech**. We use **inverted commas** (**speech marks**) to show the beginning and end of the speech, including its punctuation.

If a statement in speech comes before an explanation like 'Paolo said', the speech ends with a comma. The explanation does not use a capital letter unless it is a proper noun, like a name.

- "Here is your soup," said the waitress.
- "I hope you like it," Paul said.

Get started

Copy out each sentence and label it 'corrrect' or 'incorrect' to show whether **all** the punctuation has been used correctly. Underline the incorrect parts of the sentences. One has been done for you.

1. "Today we will be painting," Announced Mrs Blake. incorrect
2. "That sounds fun replied Katie."
3. "I can't wait to start," added Alistair.
4. "shall I get the paints?" Tariq asked.
5. Mrs Blake replied, "Yes, that would be helpful."
6. "I'm going to use lots of colours" said Katie.
7. "Use this paper," Mrs Blake instructed us.
8. Shelby said, "I wonder what we're painting."

Try these

Copy and complete these sentences by adding the correct punctuation. One has been done for you.

1. *"We are going to paint this fruit," stated Mrs Blake.*
2. I wonder if we can eat some Carrie whispered
3. Don't be so silly retorted Hasan
4. Please get started urged Mrs Blake
5. Shaul spilled the water jug squeaked Pippa
6. Perhaps you could help to clear it up Mrs Blake said calmly
7. Alistair's painting something different called Tariq
8. That's enough talking replied Mrs Blake

Now try these

Write a conversation of at least four sentences about each of these topics. Try to use speech before explanations in your conversation.

1. Two children discussing a TV programme
2. A family talking about plans for the weekend
3. A teacher telling a class about some homework
4. Children arguing about who broke something
5. Two brothers deciding how to get somewhere
6. Two sisters considering how to build something

Punctuating direct speech (2)

Inverted commas go around **direct speech**, including its punctuation. If speech needs to end in an exclamation mark or a question mark, this also goes inside the inverted commas. The speech keeps its exclamation mark or question mark whether it comes before or after an explanation like 'Jake shouted'.

After speech, the explanation still does not use a capital letter unless it is a proper noun, like a name.

- "Look behind you!" Jake shouted.

- "What is it?" asked Percie.

Get started

Copy and complete these sentences, adding punctuation at the end of the direct speech. One has been done for you.

1. *"Am I dreaming?" asked Millie, sitting back down.*

2. "What do you mean" questioned Ade.

3. "I can't believe my luck" exclaimed Millie.

4. "Did you win that art competition" Ade enquired.

5. Millie cried, "I did"

6. Ade gasped, "That's wonderful"

7. "What should I do with the prize money" wondered Millie.

8. "We could go on holiday" Ade responded gleefully.

Try these

Copy and complete these sentences, adding the correct punctuation. One has been done for you.

1. *Our teacher, Mr Cary, explained, "I have an idea for helping the community."*

2. Shall we hold a tea dance for older people he suggested

3. My gran would love that exclaimed Geoff

4. Mr Cary asked Who thinks it's a good idea

5. The children all cried out I do

6. I am pleased you agree said the teacher

7. Shall we form a planning team he enquired

8. Sandeep said I'd love to help

Now try these

Write conversations of at least six sentences between these characters, punctuating them carefully. Make sure you use questions and at least one exclamation in each one.

1. Sandeep and Geoff, planning the tea dance

2. Martin and Angus, designing a poster for the tea dance

3. Mr Cary and the class, discussing progress with the planning

4. Geoff and his grandma, as he invites her to the dance

5. Geoff's grandma and Sandeep's grandpa during the dance

6. Mr Cary and the class, talking about how it went